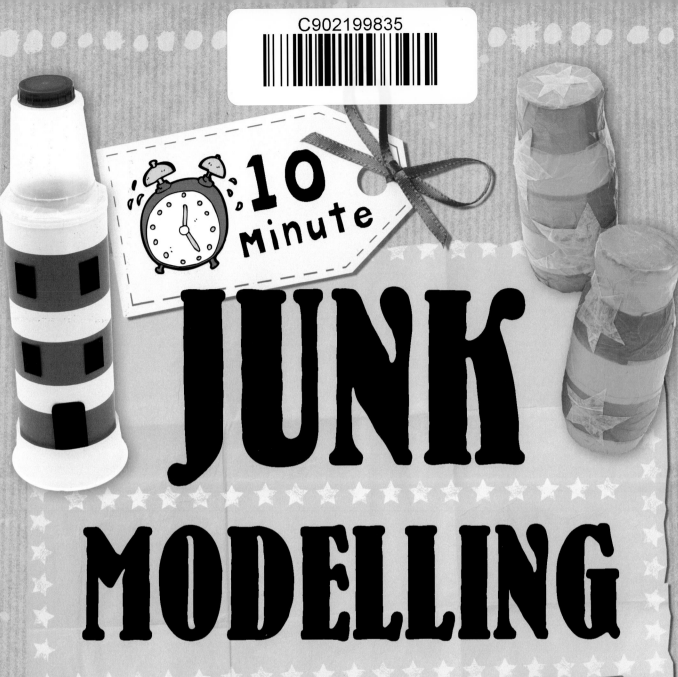

10 Minute

JUNK

MODELLING

Annalees Lim

WAYLAND

First published in paperback in 2016 by Wayland

Copyright © Wayland, 2016

Dewey Number: 745.5'84-dc23
ISBN: 978 0 7502 9703 5
10 9 8 7 6 5 4 3 2

Printed in China

FSC

Wayland
An imprint of
Hachette Children's Group
Part of Hodder & Stoughton
Carmelite House
50 Victoria Embankment
London EC4Y 0DZ

An Hachette UK Company
www.hachette.co.uk

www.hachettechildrens.co.uk

Editor: Elizabeth Brent
Craft stylist: Annalees Lim
Designer: Elaine Wilkinson
Photographer: Simon Pask, N1 Studios

The website addresses (URLs) and QR codes included in this book were valid at the time of going to press. However, it is possible that contents or addresses may have changed since the publication of this book. No responsibility for any such changes can be accepted by either the author or the Publisher.

Picture acknowledgements:
All step-by-step craft photography: Simon Pask, N1 Studios;
images used throughout for creative graphics: Shutterstock

Contents

Junk modelling

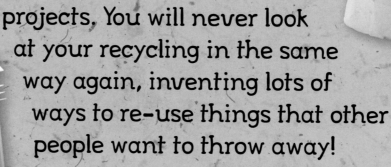

Junk modelling is one of the most creative ways of crafting. It turns things you may think of as rubbish into fabulous new projects. You will never look at your recycling in the same way again, inventing lots of ways to re-use things that other people want to throw away!

You can find the craft materials you need to make the projects in this book all around you. Before you throw anything away, check if it can be re-used — always ask a grown-up first to make sure. Look out for colourful paper from magazines, and spare buttons and ribbons from packaging, as well as boxes, plastic pots and cardboard tubes.

It is really important to make sure that all of the 'junk' is clean before you start making your projects. Clean food containers or things you find outside with warm, soapy water, remembering to leave everything to dry afterwards.

Keep all of your junk treasure together in one place so that it is ready to use whenever you want to get creative. Whatever you use to keep your modelling materials in, remember you can always decorate that too! Try newspaper collage, painting a colourful pattern on the outside, or even adding glitter to make it extra special.

Crafting can be messy, especially if you are using glitter or glue, so make sure you cover all your work surfaces with old newspaper or a plastic tablecloth before you begin. Always wash your hands after you have used glue to stop your works of art being ruined by sticky fingers, and always ask an adult to help you with sharp scissors or compasses.

Junk modelling doesn't have to stop with the projects that are in this book. Think about how you can add to the crafts. You could make a jungle for your dinosaur on pages 8—9 to live in, or a stormy sea to go around your lighthouse on pages 16—17. The options are endless, so roll up your sleeves and get crafting!

Toilet tube gift boxes

These gift boxes are perfect for special occasions. Fill them with small pieces of handmade jewellery wrapped in tissue paper, or with foil-wrapped sweet treats that you can give to someone to say 'thank you'.

1

Flatten the toilet roll.

2

Press one of the edges down and in on itself.

3

Fold the opposite edge on top of it and repeat on the other side.

4

Cut a piece of colourful paper big enough to fit around the tube. Stick down with the glue stick.

5

Cut a star shape out of coloured card and make a hole in one of the points. Thread a ribbon through it and tie the star around the middle of the box to make the tag.

These boxes also make great building blocks. Tape them together to make space ships and other machines, or cute animal characters!

Tin foil dinosaur

This tiny Triceratops is easy to make, and uses materials you can find in your kitchen cupboards. Once you've mastered the technique, try making a whole herd of dinosaurs!

1

Roll up some foil to make one large ball, one medium sized ball and four small balls.

2

Stick them together using the sticky tape to make the head, body and legs of your dinosaur.

Use the scissors to cut the cocktail sticks in half. Poke five into the top of the head in a fan shape, one in the back for the tail and then three shorter ones in the face to make the horns.

Carefully cover all of the foil and cocktail sticks with another layer of tin foil. Stick it down with the glue stick if needed, and add the googly eyes.

Use neat paint to colour the tin foil and then leave it to dry completely. This may take several hours.

You could also make a forest or a nest out of tin foil, for your dinosaur to live in.

Tin can robot

Robots are usually built from wires and circuit boards. This metal pal is much simpler to make, but just as helpful. Your tin robot can hold all your notes and remind you of the things you need to do.

1

Stick the small tin can to the top of the larger one with sticky pads.

2

Cut out two 2 cmx6 cm rectangles and two 2.5 cmx2.5 cm squares from the silver card to make the robot's arms and legs. Stick a magnet to the end of each one using the sticky pads.

3

Cut out two circles of silver card, slightly bigger than the googly eyes. Stick the eyes to them, then stick them to the robot's face with sticky pads.

4

Make a card circuit-board belly with buttons made from electrical tape, and attach a magnet to the back with a sticky pad. Add stripes to the body using the electrical tape.

5

Attach all of the magnets to the tin can. Use them to stick notes or pictures to the robot's body.

Tin cans are a great material to use but they can be sharp. Always ask an adult to help you prepare the tin first by soaking off any labels and covering sharp edges with sticky tape.

Cardboard castle

You will need:
- A square tissue box
- scissors
- wrapping paper
- double-sided tape
- 4 cardboard tubes
- scrap paper
- craft foam

Your junk castle will be so impressive that you'll want to build an entire crafty kingdom from cardboard!

1

Remove the top of the tissue box, leaving the bottom and sides intact.

2

Cover the box with the wrapping paper, and fix it in place with the double-sided tape.

3

Cut the tubes so they are a bit taller than the box and cover them in scrap paper. Cut into the tops of the tubes and the box to make the turrets.

4

Stick strips of double-sided tape to the foam. Cut out small brick shapes and long strips from the foam, then stick them to the box and turrets.

5

Tape your castle together, and stick a big foam door to the front.

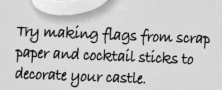

Try making flags from scrap paper and cocktail sticks to decorate your castle.

Plastic bottle plane

You will need:
- A 500ml plastic bottle
- scissors
- 3 lolly sticks
- A paper cup
- Sticky tape
- cardboard
- Black and white electrical tape

Plastic bottles are thrown away every day, so why not recycle one into an aeroplane? You can use it to jet around finding more junk to re-use!

1

Lay the bottle on its side, and make a small slit in each side of the front of it using the scissors. Push a lolly stick through, then do the same at the back and top of the bottle.

2

Cut the paper cup in half and tape the bottom part to the bottom of the bottle.

3

Cut out some cardboard wings and fins, and stick them to the lolly sticks using sticky tape.

4

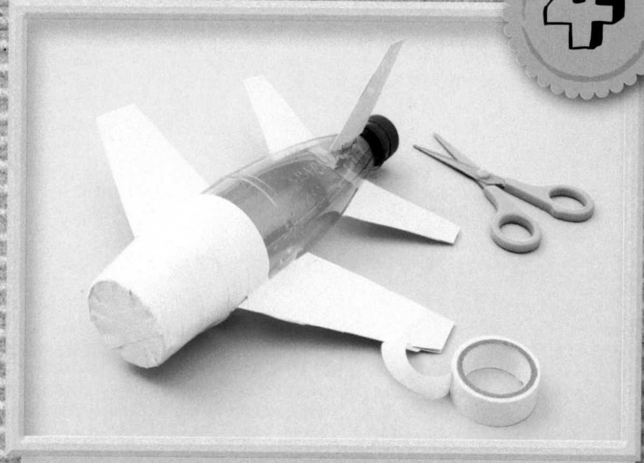

Cover the whole thing with a layer of white electrical tape.

5

Cut out small window shapes from the black electrical tape and stick them to each side of the plane.

Why not attach some string to the plane so you can hang it from the ceiling and make it look as if it is soaring around?

Crisp tube lighthouse

You will need:

- A crisp tube and lid
- A small, clear yoghurt pot
- Sticky tape
- Red and black scrap paper
- Scissors
- Double-sided tape
- A large yoghurt pot
- A plastic bottle top

You can find lighthouses all around the world, each one slightly different from the next. Make yours really special by making it all from recycled materials.

1

Use the sticky tape to fix the clear yoghurt pot to the crisp tube lid.

2

Cover the crisp tube with the red paper, fixing it in place with the sticky tape.

3

Use the double-sided tape to make stripes all the way up the tube, making sure you don't peel off the paper layer.

4

Make windows and a door from the black paper, and stick them onto the tube using double-sided tape. Put the lid on the tube.

5

Cut the bottom and rim off the large yoghurt pot. Stick the rim to the base of the lighthouse. Stick the bottle lid to the yoghurt pot bottom, and stick both to the top of the lighthouse.

Real lighthouses use bright lamps to guide ships. If you are feeling really creative, don't glue down the lid of the lighthouse so that you can put a torch inside the crisp tube and light it up.

Tin foil toadstool

Toadstools can be found in most forests but should be looked at and not touched. Make your own toadstool to keep inside and play with whenever you want.

1

Scrunch some foil up into a stalk shape, with one pointed end.

2

Cut out a section of the egg box and cover it in layers of foil to make the toadstool cap.

3

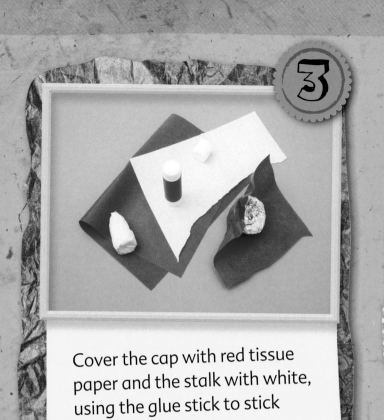

Cover the cap with red tissue paper and the stalk with white, using the glue stick to stick the paper down.

4

Use the glue stick to stick the cap to the stalk.

5

Cut out some small circles from the white paper and stick them onto the toadstool cap.

Make lots of toadstools of different sizes, to create a whole fantasy forest!

Mini musical shaker

You will need:

- A yoghurt drink pot
- card
- A pencil
- Scissors
- A funnel
- Rice
- Sticky tape
- Double-sided tape
- Plastic bags, in different colours

You can fill these shakers with any rice, dried beans or pulses you can find. If you don't have any lying around, try cutting up a plastic pot into bits to use instead.

1

Draw around the top of the yoghurt drink pot on card to make a lid, then cut it out.

2

Fill the yoghurt drink pot one-third full of rice, using the funnel to help you.

3

Tape the card lid to the top of the yoghurt drink pot, making sure it is very secure.

4

Stick double-sided tape to two of the plastic bags. Cut the strips out and wrap them around the shaker, alternating the colours until the whole bottle is covered.

5

Stick strips of double-sided tape onto another plastic bag and cut out small star shapes. Stick them to the shaker to decorate it.

Make a whole band of instruments so that you can play with other people. Add some elastic bands to an open box that you can pluck like a harp, or decorate an old biscuit tin to make into a drum.

Paper plate owl

You will need:
- 2 paper plates
- Scissors
- Tissue paper strips
- A glue stick
- Scrap paper
- Googly eyes

You'll have such a hoot making these cute owls that you won't want to stop at just making one!

1

Cut one of the paper plates in half, then cut one of the halves into wing shapes.

2

Cut the rim off the other half-plate, to make the owl's tummy.

3

Fold the tissue paper strips into concertinas and cut them into 'u' shapes. Open them up to make feathers, and glue these to the wings, ears and tummy.

4

Cut an '8' shape for the eyes and some feet and a beak out of scrap paper. Stick on the googly eyes.

5

Glue the wings, ears, tummy, eyes, beak and feet to the plain paper plate.

These little owls look great on their own, but if you make lots you can string them up to make colourful bunting.

Glossary

acrylic paint thick paint that can be mixed with water

bunting a row of small paper or cloth decorations on a string

invent to be the first person to think or to make something

kingdom a country ruled by a king or queen

neat not mixed with water

pulses dried seeds such as peas, beans or lentils that can be eaten

technique a way of doing something

Index